SCANDINAVIA

This is the second book to be published in
this series. The author draws upon his own
long periods of geographical field study
within this area of peninsulas and islands.
A vivid and stimulating impression of these
unique lands is outlined by a text which
allows the development of certain significant
scenes and topics in detail, while at the same
time giving a lead to the broader survey.
Since it is hoped that the reader will
throughout this series be developing a
geographical approach, new techniques and
a wider vocabulary, there are features
deliberately included within the text and/or
illustrative maps, diagrams and pictures
which are different from those used in *South
Asia*. Many of these features will suggest
new ways of "finding out."
As with *South Asia*, the author, artist and
designer have collaborated carefully to make
the book up-to-date and meaningful, while
at the same time attractive and interesting to
use.

FINDING OUT
ABOUT GEOGRAPHY

Art Editors
Colin Banks and
John Miles

Illustrated by Zena Flax

GOLDEN PRESS · NEW YORK

Scandinavia

By ROBERT CLAYTON

Published by Golden Press Inc., New York

Printed in the USA
by Western Printing
and Lithographing Company

Library of Congress Catalog Card Number
67-17969

CONTENTS

The influence of the sea	6	Farming in Denmark	30
Fjord life in Norway	8	Iceland and Greenland	34
Sources of power in the different countries	15	Industries of Scandinavia	38
		Tourism	42
The forests	19	Scandinavian cities	43
Fishing	24	Scandinavian trade	46
Ice action in the Ice Age and today	28	Glossary	48

A Viking ship now in Oslo museum

Whaling in the Arctic in the early nineteenth century

A modern passenger ferry 'Allotar'

In few other parts of the world do rivers, lakes, seas and oceans play so great a part in the lives of the people. No wonder the old Norse saying "The land divides us; the sea unites us" is often heard in these countries. A glance at the world map shows some of this influence, but only on a map of a large scale is it possible to show all of the many lakes, rivers and small islands which exist. Ice-sheets, *glaciers* and high mountains cover much of these northerly countries, and so most of the people live on the flatter land around lowland lakes and near to the coastline.

Over a thousand years ago the *Vikings* knew these seas and oceans well enough to sail westwards to the British Isles, Iceland, Greenland and even to America, while some of their ships reached southern Europe and the Black Sea. These ancient skills in navigation and ship-building have been handed down from father to son, so that today their large merchant fleets, flying the Scandinavian flags, are known all over the world. A small Danish short-sea trader from Esbjerg unloads butter and bacon at a berth alongside London Bridge; a huge Norwegian oil tanker fills its hold at a Texan port. The world's largest whaling fleet is Norwegian, and it must travel over 8,000 miles to reach the Antarctic seas for the summer whaling season (November–February). The world's first diesel ship was the "Selandia", built in 1912 by the Copenhagen firm Burmeister and Wain.

6

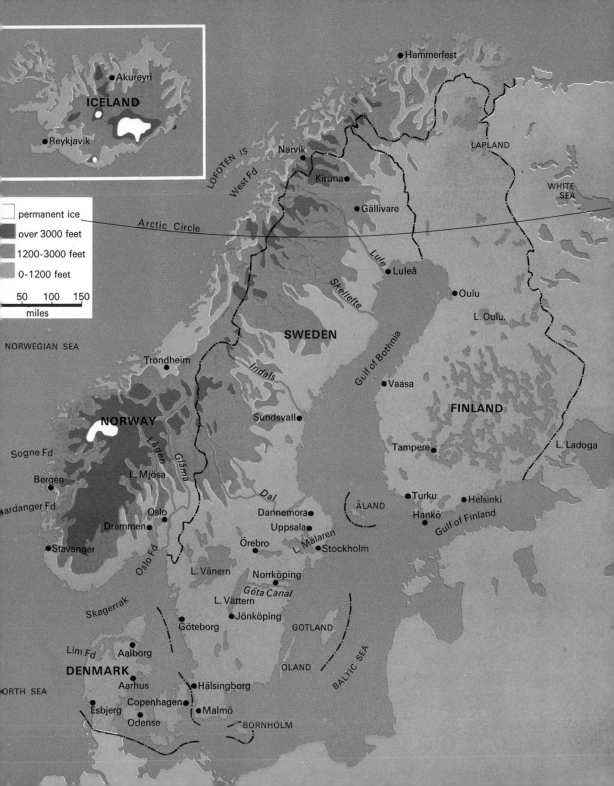

Many of the large cargo liners rarely return home. They move from one world port to another handling trade for other countries. But around the long indented coastlines of Scandinavian countries small local vessels carry people and items of trade from port to port, from village to village.

The long, deep *fjords* of western Norway are often the only lines of communication for the farmers who live here. Most of these men own their own small motorboat, and their cargo from the farm may be milk, cheese, cherries, cattle, sheep or pigs. For the return, the cargo may be gas, diesel oil, livestock fodder, groceries, farm machinery or the mail.

Right: Geiranger fjord in Norway

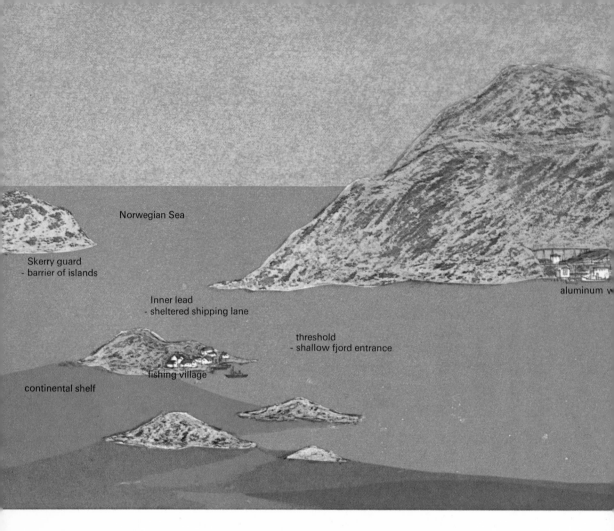

Norwegian Sea

Skerry guard - barrier of islands

Inner lead - sheltered shipping lane

threshold - shallow fjord entrance

aluminum w

fishing village

continental shelf

The diagram shows the way each part of the fjord landscape can be used to provide a livelihood for the Norwegians of this area. As the seasons change so the jobs that need doing change, and for each member of the family the jobs are different. The farmer and his son will plow the tiny, sloping fields near the farm, and later plant potatoes, oats and turnips. While they are working in these fields or taking hay down from a steeper field, the daughter may be at the *saeter,* the farmer's high mountain pasture, where the dairy cows graze in the summer months.

The saeter girls milk the cows and make cheese. The small huts they live in are just above the forest and are made of logs and roofed with turf. Some of the huts are no longer used: the mountain pasture is fenced and sheep are there in place of the cattle. The girls are needed down in the valley to pick the fruit in the enlarged orchards. Most of them are not sorry to leave the lonely saeter huts.

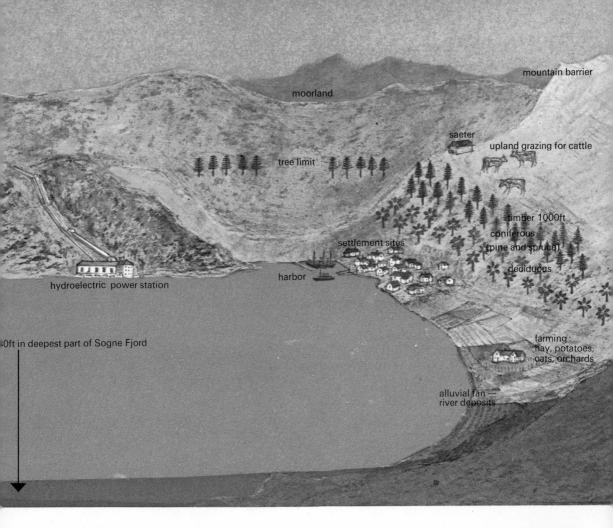

mountain barrier

moorland

saeter

upland grazing for cattle

tree limit

timber 1000ft
coniferous
(pine and spruce)

settlement sites

deciduous

harbor

hydroelectric power station

farming:
hay, potatoes,
oats, orchards

0ft in deepest part of Sogne Fjord

alluvial fan —
river deposits

Tromsö : A typical small
town on the edge of
a fjord

Norway in the winter.
Notice the long shadows. At this time of
year daylight does not last long

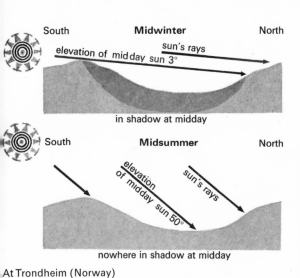

South   **Midwinter**   North

elevation of midday sun 3°   sun's rays

in shadow at midday

South   **Midsummer**   North

elevation of midday sun 50°   sun's rays

nowhere in shadow at midday

At Trondheim (Norway)
approximate latitude 63° 30′ N

The forest of pine and spruce provides a winter job for the men when the ground is hard, the land snow covered and the animals indoors. The days are short at this season, and the sun only rises a short distance in the sky. On the southern side of the valley the land is in shadow even at midday. Further north, beyond the *Arctic Circle*, there are days when the sun never rises. In summer there are days when the sun never sets.

Fishing is another occupation for the fjord farmer. Just as he has pasture rights on the high moorland, so he has fishing rights on part of the fjord. Later we will look at those for whom fishing is a full-time job.

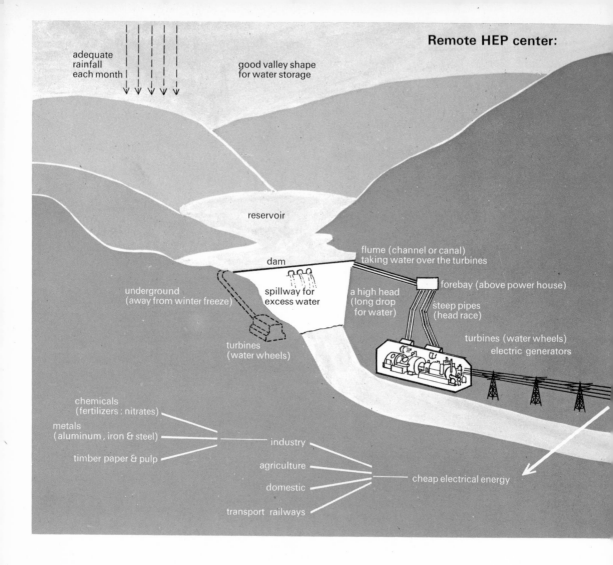

Remote HEP center:

adequate rainfall each month

good valley shape for water storage

reservoir

dam

flume (channel or canal) taking water over the turbines

forebay (above power house)

underground (away from winter freeze)

spillway for excess water

a high head (long drop for water)

steep pipes (head race)

turbines (water wheels)

turbines (water wheels) electric generators

chemicals (fertilizers : nitrates)

metals (aluminum, iron & steel)

timber paper & pulp

industry

agriculture

domestic

cheap electrical energy

transport railways

One thing that is rarely lacking at the fjord farm, or anywhere in Scandinavia for that matter, is electricity. Many villages have their own hydroelectric plants, but elsewhere huge power stations supply electricity for *grids* which serve homes and industries.

Peat is available in all the Scandinavian countries, but only in the Faeroes and in Iceland is it a major fuel. Coal is chiefly mined in west Greenland and in Norway's Spitsbergen fields. In Sweden, Norway and Finland timber is plentiful and often provides the fuel for the large kitchen stoves. But it is to hydroelectric stations that these countries look for their major source of power. Even Denmark has one or two small hydroelectric power

Above : A hydroelectric power station at
Rødberg in Norway (65 miles N W of Oslo)

Right : The discharge tunnel for water in Sweden's
biggest hydroelectric power station at
Stornorrforsen. The tunnel is the largest
of its kind in the world

stations, while a cable below the Sound brings
a small extra supply from Sweden. The rapid
increase in metal and chemical industries in
these countries is largely due to this cheap
power supply. Thus water is again helping to
change the lives of the people. The large sawmills of Sweden and Finland depend upon
this source of power.

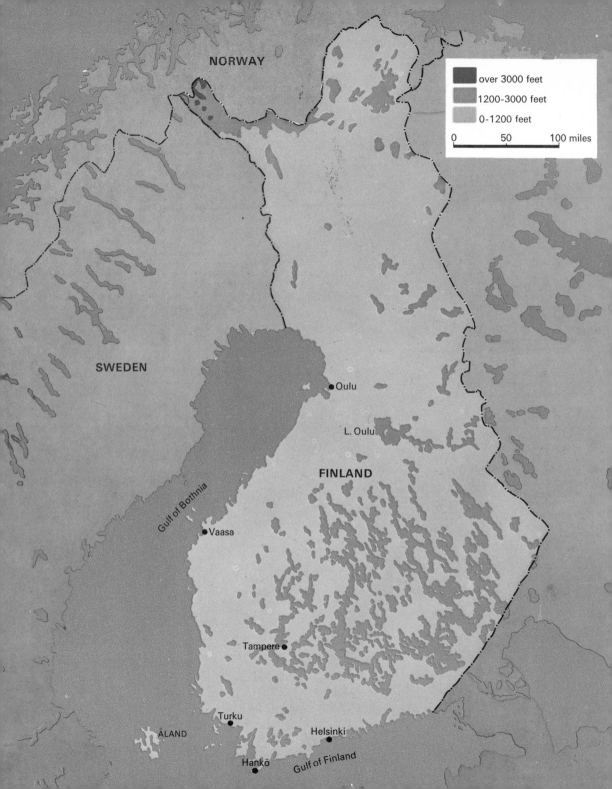

NORWAY

SWEDEN

over 3000 feet

1200-3000 feet

0-1200 feet

0   50   100 miles

Oulu

L. Oulu

FINLAND

Gulf of Bothnia

Vaasa

Tampere

Turku

ÅLAND

Helsinki

Hankö

Gulf of Finland

Seven-tenths of Finland is forested (the highest proportion of any country in the world); over half of Sweden is forested; the proportion in Norway is a fifth.

The autumn and winter are usually the tree felling seasons. Felling is easier when the sap is low, but the chief advantage is the frozen ground over which it is much easier to drag the logs or pull them along on sleds. The logs are stacked by the waterways to await the thaw.

Finland is further east than any other part of Scandinavia, but even here some of the warming influence of the *North Atlantic Drift* which affects all Scandinavia is felt. In spring and early summer the frozen rivers and lakes melt, first in the south, and then these waterways become the log floatways. Sometimes the logs are tied together to form rafts which can be towed to the saw mill by a tug; sometimes the logs float freely down the river with only a wooden barrier along the river edge to stop them catching in the shallow water obstructions. There are thousands of miles of floatways. Even forests in the center of the country are within reach of this cheap means of transport.

Huge islands of timber wait in the water alongside the sawmills. When steam power was first used in the sawmills in the 1860's it was obvious that the best site for a mill was near the coast in easy reach of the imported coal. Hydroelectric power has replaced steam power in the 20th Century.

Left: Ways of transporting logs on water
Norway *(left),* A tug towing a float of logs held by
a single rope
Sweden *(below left),* A log floatway, the logs drift
with the current
Finland *(below right),* A tug towing bundles of logs

Right: Handling timber
Finland *(right),* Pushing logs down a floatway
Sweden *(below left),* Barking a tree
Norway *(below right),* Felling a tree using a
powered handsaw

Finland : Constructing a
timber house

Sweden : A farmhouse built on the
same principle as the one opposite

Left : Sweden
wooden boat houses

Below : Iceland
wooden houses with turf roofs
also a wooden church

Electric saws cut the logs into planks which later go to the large timber ports along the Gulf of Bothnia and the Gulf of Finland.

Not all the timber is exported as planks. In the mid-19th Century the way to make paper from wood pulp was discovered. Today paper, pulp, plywood, matches and furniture are manufactured in many of the Scandinavian countries. The furniture is world famous for its design.

It is not surprising that most of the houses in Scandinavia are built of wood. Many trains use wood as the fuel. It is so bulky that the train must stop every two hours to take on another load. But fire can also be a great danger where there are trees and wooden buildings. Because of this, many Scandinavian towns have been burnt down, often more than once. When rebuilding, the people have taken the opportunity to replan their towns, so today most of them look modern and conveniently laid out. In the forests great care is taken to prevent fire. Nine-tenths of Finland's exports and one-third of Sweden's are forest products, so it is no wonder that they guard the timber carefully.

A means of livelihood which is common throughout all Scandinavia, and which is also dependent upon the water areas, is fishing. The farmer-fishermen of the Norwegian fjords fish on a small scale, but from many of the ports round the North Sea, Norwegian Sea and North Atlantic Ocean long-distance fishing fleets sail out to reap "the harvest of the sea." Many experts, such as those of the *F.A.O.*, think there would be less starvation in the world if more of our food was taken from the sea, but the seas around Scandinavia, though very rich in fish, tend to suffer from over-fishing. Fish are certainly an important item in the diet of Scandinavians.

Norway exports huge quantities of herrings, cod and various manufactured goods such as animal food, fats and oil which are all made from fish. For the Faeroe Islands, Greenland and Iceland fishing is the one vital industry. It was a matter of life and death for Iceland when in the 1950's her attempt to extend the *territorial waters* around her coastline was opposed by other countries. But the 12 mile fishing limits were recognized, and so Iceland was able to gain control over valuable breeding and fishing grounds.

The two chief types of fishing here are *trawling* and *drifting*. For the fish which live on or near the sea bed (cod, plaice, haddock) a trawl net is used. Stout vessels are needed to sail the long distances, sometimes in rough

25

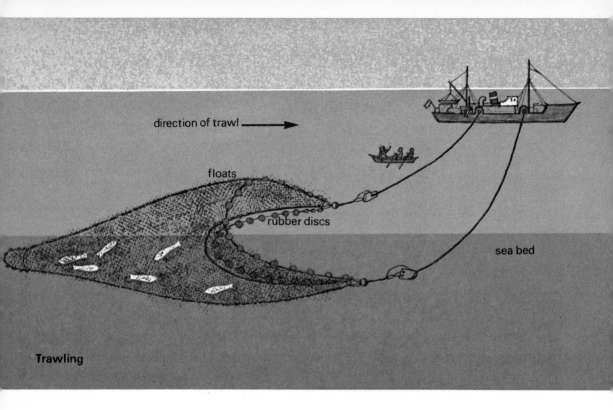

direction of trawl ⟶

floats

rubber discs

sea bed

Trawling

seas, to the cod fishing grounds. The spring season is most important (January to April). Once the long experienced ship's captain decides he is in a good area, the trawl net is let out into the sea, and for two or three hours it is towed behind. Hauling the net in is aided by the machinery on board, a cord is pulled to release the captured fish, and then the net is put back in the sea again. Throughout each day and night fishing continues until the ship has a good load to bring back to port. This journey may last a day or two, or as much as a fortnight if the fishing has been in very distant northern waters. The fishing grounds in the extreme north are almost 2,000 miles away.

The fish which swim nearer the surface (herring, mackerel) are best caught in *seine* or drift nets. Though herring may be caught at any time of the year, there is usually one good season for each area. No one knows exactly why the fish migrate as they do, but at certain times between spring and autumn they move towards the land to spawn, and this becomes the best fishing season. For the Faeroes the months are June and July; for Iceland, July and August; for Norwegians in the North Sea the season is July to October. Many of the drifters use the *echo sounder* to tell if they are over a herring shoal. The drift net is let out at night when the herrings rise in search of food. The net hangs like a curtain in the sea and stretches for about one and a half miles ahead of its ship. The net's mesh has to be of a certain size: small enough to trap the fish as

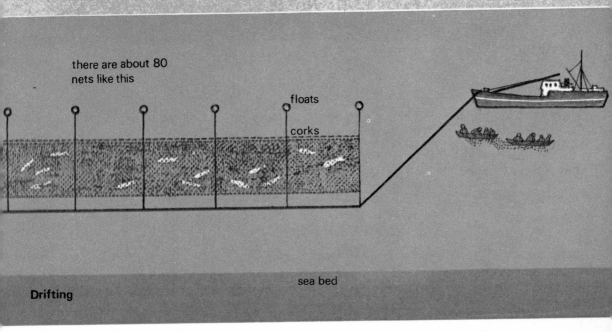

there are about 80
nets like this

floats

corks

sea bed

Drifting

their gills catch in it, but large enough to let the small, young fish pass through. In the early morning the net is hauled in, and then the drifter rushes to port to catch the best prices at the market. Most drifters aim to return to the fishing grounds the same day.

Some of the fish are rushed from the port to be sold in the markets of the large inland towns; some go to factories where they are put into deep-freeze packets which many house-wives find very convenient; some are salted and dried to make them easier to export to the warm Mediterranean countries. Some ships are now being used which are equipped for both trawling and drifting, and also on board is all the machinery necessary to clean, pack and quick freeze the fish.

'Klipfisk', the Norwegian name given to split, salted, pressed and dried cod, laying on the rocks to dry

27

Fishing is a difficult and dangerous job. Even the drifters that keep to the shallow waters of the *continental shelf* have to take great care in rough seas and when near rocky coasts. The trawlers which go far north may often have rougher seas, fog or icebergs to beware of. Though ice closes ports in the Gulf of Bothnia in winter and though it lies permanently over large areas of Iceland and most of Greenland, there was a time when it covered much more of Scandinavia: in the *Great Ice Age*.

Glaciers, like those which still move slowly from the Greenland ice sheet down to the coast, once flowed down most of the Scandinavian valleys. Their great mass, mixed with hard rock boulders, wore down the valleys. Some were deepened to below sea level, and so when the ice melted, the sea moved in to give the long inlets we now know as fjords. In the higher areas the movement of ice eroded the rocks: in the lower areas the glaciers have left behind the crushed rubble that they had carried.

One interesting change since the Ice Ages has been the movement of the mainland area of Scandinavia. The great weight of ice had caused the land to sink: as the ice melted so the land began to rise again. The effect is rather like a large flat cork floating on water. Place a weight on the cork and it sinks, take off the weight and the cork rises again.

As this uplift of land has taken place around Norway and Sweden, large, fairly flat areas of land have risen from below the sea. Here many of the people live and farm today.

Left : A glacier in
Iceland. In the foreground
the glacier is depositing
its morainic load

Right : Stockholm
harbor in early spring.
The ice is beginning
to break up

A typical fishing
settlement on glacial
deposits that have risen above
sea level since
the Great Ice Age

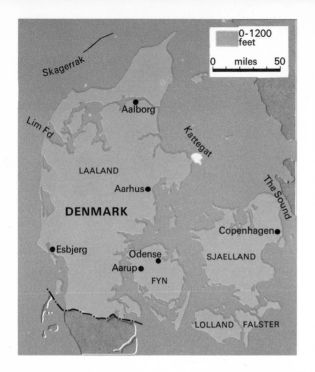

Denmark is a low, yet undulating country that is covered by the material left when the ice cover melted: sands, gravels and clays. Though the Danish people themselves are like many other Scandinavians, their land is very different: here is a landscape that has been made into rich agricultural land.

Denmark used to export wheat, but its small farms could not compete with the huge export of wheat that arrived in Europe from North America in the latter part of the 19th Century. So it was that the Danish arable land changed to the production of fodder for cattle and pigs, and the cattle were bred with one aim in mind: high milk yields. Today Denmark is famous

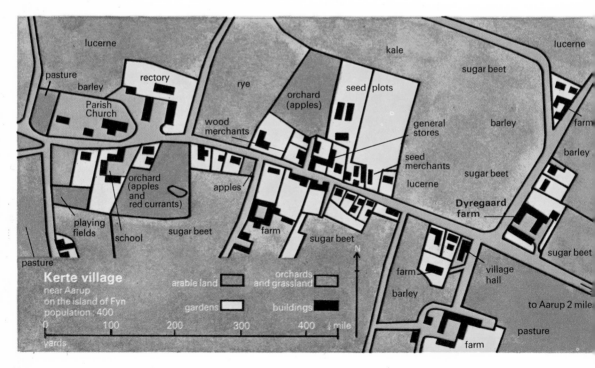

Kerte village
near Aarup
on the island of Fyn
population: 400

| | arable land | | orchards and grassland | |
| | gardens | | buildings | |

0   100   200   300   400   ½ mile
yards

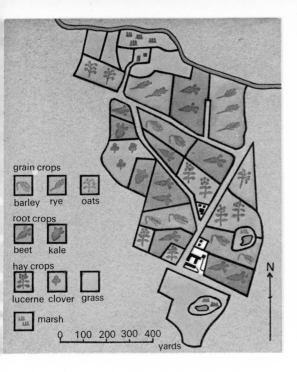

grain crops

barley rye oats

root crops

beet kale

hay crops

lucerne clover grass

marsh

0 100 200 300 400
yards

N

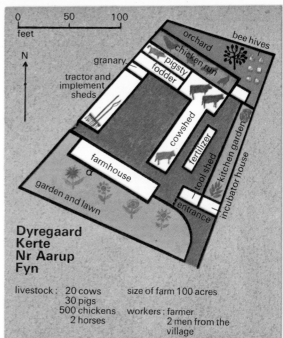

0 50 100
feet

N

orchard bee hives

granary chicken run

tractor and pigsty
implement fodder
sheds

cowshed

fertilizer

tool shed

kitchen garden

farmhouse

garden and lawn entrance

incubator house

**Dyregaard
Kerte
Nr Aarup
Fyn**

livestock: 20 cows   size of farm 100 acres
          30 pigs
          500 chickens workers: farmer
          2 horses   2 men from the
                                  village

for its dairy produce: butter, bacon, eggs and cheese – in particular for the items to be found on the British breakfast table.

The pictures, diagrams and maps alongside show what is happening in a typical Danish farming area. The village of Aarup is on the island of Fyn. Each farm is quite small and has pigs, chickens and about 15 to 20 cattle. The rotation system is of crops which provide the best food for the livestock. In many respects the landscape is like many of the lowland areas of Britain. But the farm buildings are different, and the red and white flag which flies at most Danish homes makes the difference clear.

To help with the change to dairying the cooperative movement was begun in Denmark in the 1880's. The farmers decided that their produce would be processed and sold by the

**Typical
rotation**
years

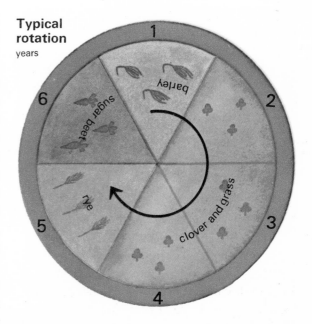

barley

1

sugar beet

6

2

clover and grass

rye

5

3

4

31

A typical cooperative dairy farm. Notice the
loading bays in front of the building

A few windmills are still to be
seen in the Danish farm landscape

best methods if they did it themselves – in
dairies, slaughter houses or factories that they
borrowed money to build. They have kept
control of this work and have always made
certain that the standard of butter, bacon and
cheese produced is kept very high. Often one
or two of the Danish farmers' older children
work part time at such factories. The cooperative movement works for the farmers in
many other ways: improving grain seed,
organizing agricultural shows, breeding bulls
to improve the stock, etc.

Each farm has a good selection of machinery
to save time and money and often to do a task
better than the farmer can do it on his own.
There are only a few farms without a tractor,
and in the cowshed there is modern equipment
to milk the cows and to cool the milk before it
goes into the large cans which are collected by
a truck from the large dairy in the nearby town.

Near to the farmhouse is a large fruit and
vegetable garden in which the farmer and his

wife grow much of the food they eat. Danes
are very fond of apples, pears, black and red
currants and strawberries, and these will be
grown in the orchard. Notice how the farm
buildings often form an open square shape.
This is useful for keeping in the livestock and
the poultry. The cattle are not often outside,
though sometimes they may be put into a
field to eat the crop there. Then an electric
fence is put around them to make certain they
do not eat too much; but more often than not
the cattle are kept in the cowshed so that all the
fields can grow their maximum amount of food
in the summer months.

Though farming, forestry, fishing and
mining are important occupations for many
Scandinavians, most of the people today live in
urban areas and most of the urban areas of
these countries are ports. Here they are busy
with the trade of their country and with the
increasing number of industries that have
developed.

In Iceland's capital, Reykjavik, is one-third of the island's population. Here also in south-west Iceland are the island's only extensive fertile lowland areas. This is therefore where most of the cattle are reared and where the hay crop is richest. Reykjavik has attracted many people from the rural areas to swell its modern suburbs. The chief industries of the capital are connected with fishing, but others are starting. Apart from hydroelectric power, there are hot springs and mud volcanoes a little inland which may one day be used more for industry. The hot springs are already used for heating greenhouses, domestic central heating and the swimming bath. (The volcanic activity in Iceland was in the world news again in the 1960's when a new volcanic island suddenly grew up out of the sea in the Vestmannaeyjar group in the south.)

Only the southern coastal fringes of Greenland are free from a cover of permanent ice. Here the total population is only about 25,000, and hence it is not surprising to find few industries. Fishing is the basic industry. The few skilled engineers and scientists who do live in Greenland are nearly all connected with the *meteorological* stations and the United States defense stations there. The important position of Greenland between major world countries can best be seen by looking down onto the globe.

A volcanic landscape
Hveragerdir, a small Icelandic village
which has grown up around hot springs.
Steam from the springs can be seen in
the circle below

The crater of a small volcano
near Myvatn in Iceland

ananas growing in a hothouse in Iceland ;
ater from natural hot springs

elandic farmers shearing sheep

Below : Whaling, cutting the meat away
from a whale's bone

Minerals

Co   coal
Cop copper (pyrite)
Go   gold
Ir   iron
Man manganese
Mo   molybdenum
Ni   nickel
Si   silver
Ti   titanium
Z   zinc

Main industrial centers

A   aluminum
Ce   cement
Ch   chemicals
E   electrical equipment
F   fish processing
Gl   glassware
IS   iron and steel
Mac machinery
P   paper and pulp
Sh   shipbuilding
Te   textiles
V   various electrochemical
     and electrometallurgical

An iron ore mine in North Sweden

It is in the other Scandinavian countries that industry plays a more important part in the lives of the people. Shipbuilding has already been mentioned, and reference has been made to the many industries based upon agricultural products, timber resources and fish.

Smaller but important manufacturing industries are those of bricks, building stone, electrical machines and textiles. Denmark is famous for its cement (at Aalborg), for beer and for the beautiful ware produced by the Royal Danish Porcelain Factory at Copenhagen. The metal industries of Norway make use of both local ores and the plentiful supply of hydroelectric power.

Sweden is the most industrialized of all the Scandinavian countries, and though there is great variety (glass, earthenware, flour milling, textiles, sugar and oil refining in the south, for example), it is the iron and steel industry which stands out as the most important.

For over a hundred years Sweden has been a great exporter of iron ore. At first ore came from the area to the north of the low, lake-covered central region of Sweden which lies inland from the capital city, Stockholm. In those days the ore was partly refined using charcoal as the source of heat to melt it. The huge iron fields of northern Sweden (Kiruna and Malmberget) could only begin production when a process to remove this iron's impurities

39

was invented. This discovery was made in 1879 and from then onwards these northern areas have exported great quantities of ore.

Your map will show you that these areas are both north of the Arctic Circle: the latitude of northern Alaska, and further north than Iceland. It is not easy to work here because of the winter snow cover and long dark days. To the north is Lapland, a lower area which runs across several countries and takes its name from the nomadic *Lapps* who live here. Some of them have sold their reindeer herds and settled in these new mining towns where it is easy to get a job. They do not mind the cold, dark days as much as the Swedes who have come north from central Sweden.

Fortunately much of the mining is underground where it is warmer. Electric trains run through the many miles of tunnel carrying the ore to the surface. Larger electric trains carry the ore from the iron fields north to the Norwegian port of Narvik or south to the Swedish port of Lulea. The ore arriving at Lulea has to wait there in the winter, for the Gulf of Bothnia is frozen then for about four months. Though Narvik is further north, it is kept ice free in winter by the North Atlantic Drift, and so ore export can continue. But snow sheds, tunnels and wooden barriers have had to be built along the railway to Narvik, because the thick snow on the high land can easily slip down to block the track.

It is the ore from Sweden that is exported to the large iron towns of western Europe. Some goes to the United States. In some of the large towns of central and southern Sweden important industries are based on this ore from the north. A great variety of iron and steel products are made, varying in size from small ball bearings to huge girders.

It is also not surprising to find in many Swedish farming villages both a sawmill and a small iron works. This type of village is particularly common in the low central region where the farming is largely based on hay and cattle.

Left : Lapland. Besides the industries in the North
ne of the main sources of food and clothing
s the reindeer. Here they are being rounded up

Below : A modern Swedish brickworks. The
temperature is so high that the workers have
to wear asbestos suits

Below : A glassworker in Southern Sweden

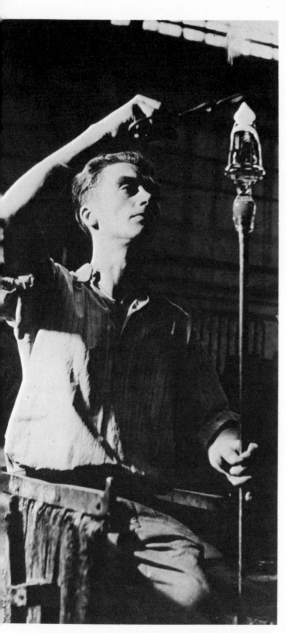

An industry so far not mentioned is that of tourism. All the Scandinavian countries are trying to earn more money by tempting people to come for their holidays to see the interesting things there are. You may be able to think of quite a few places of interest from what you have read so far in this book: the beautiful fjords of Norway, with the nearby mountains attracting skiers to their snow-covered slopes in winter; geysers, glaciers and volcanic scenery in Iceland; the Lapp or Eskimo country where people's lives, their clothes, their building materials and food are so obviously controlled by the severe climate. Other tourists like to look at the country and the birthplace of famous people, and Scandinavia has had a good share of these: writers have included Hans Christian Andersen, the children's story writer, who was born in Odense on the Danish island of Fyn in 1805; the Norwegian dramatist Hendrik Ibsen, born in 1828; and the Swedish poet and dramatist, Johan August Strindberg who was born in Stockholm in 1849. In the world of music many will know of the Norwegian Edvard Grieg, born in the fishing port of Bergen in 1843. He used much of the folk music of the country in his compositions, for example, in the music to Ibsen's "Peer Gynt." Other composers of note are Johan Julius Sibelius born at Tavastehus in Finland and Carl Nielsen, probably Denmark's greatest composer. Both these composers were born in the same year, 1865. Like Andersen, Nielsen was born on the island of Fyn.

It is not surprising to find that Scandinavians have often been great explorers and travelers: the Norwegians Nansen (born 1861) and Amundsen (born 1872) explored in polar areas, the former in the north. Amundsen planned to go to the North Pole, but having heard that the American Peary was there, he set off south to Antarctica to reach the South Pole just before Scott. Thor Heyerdahl's "Kon-Tiki" raft which crossed the Pacific Ocean is proudly preserved in his country's capital. There are many more who deserve mention but space is limited.

It is to the Scandinavian cities that most tourists come. Many of these cities are extremely beautiful and they are noted for being clean and well planned. One of the commonest events in the history of most Scandinavian towns has been destruction by fire: Bergen, Oslo, Helsinki, Stockholm, Göteborg and many others too, sometimes more than once. It is not surprising that this should have happened where most of the houses are of wood, and where large log fires burn inside to keep out the winter cold. One advantage of the destruction by fire has been the opportunity of replanning flattened areas.

Like most of the large Scandinavian cities Oslo is a port, and like most Norwegian ports Oslo is situated on flat land by the sheltered but deep water of a fjord. It grew as a trading center, supplying the needs of the rich lowland areas to either side and the many valleys

Hans Christian Andersen

August Strindberg

Edvard Grieg

Amundsen

Thor Heyerdahl

which open to the Oslo Fjord. To the trading, industry has been added in the last hundred years – particularly metal, timber and dairy produce industries.

Stockholm has twice the number of inhabitants of Oslo. It also grew as a trading center for the lowland area nearby, land which has risen very slowly from below sea level (about 13 feet since A.D. 1000). Though it can be ice-bound for one or two months each winter, it has grown rapidly as a port during the last fifty years, and has become world famous for the products of its electrical engineering industry – telephones, refrigerators, vacuum cleaners, etc. Many of its one million inhabitants live on the wooded slopes to the north and south of the sea inlet or on the islands there, over which Stockholm has gradually spread in recent years. A speedy electric train system links up with the city underground lines to bring the workers in from these suburbs.

Like Stockholm, Helsinki, the capital of Finland, has spilled over from its restricted site to many of the nearby islands. Though icebound for up to four months each year, Helsinki is the chief of Finland's many ports, and ice breakers can normally keep the harbors open. Helsinki is also the country's major industrial city (machine shops, textile mills, shipyards, food, clothing, chemical and pottery factories). Timber buildings are common in the suburbs, and most of the summer bungalows on the islands are also built of wood; but the impressive government and commercial buildings of the well-planned central area are built of stone and brick. The indented Helsinki peninsula, though extremely convenient for shipping, makes urban expansion difficult, and modern blocks of apartments help to use the land efficiently.

About 2 per cent of Helsinki's inhabitants are Swedish speaking, but the percentage is decreasing; and most of these people can also speak Finnish, a language which is eastern European rather than Scandinavian. The Swedish influence, also in west Finnish towns and the Aland Islands, reflects the five and a half centuries of Swedish control lasting till 1809 A.D.

Copenhagen is by far the largest Scandinavian city. Greater Copenhagen has well over a million and a half people – one quarter of the

otal Danish population. Eight hundred years
go there were just a few huts by the small
harbor which the herring smacks and merchant ships found useful for shelter from the
tormy seas that sometimes blew up suddenly
as they sailed through the narrow Sound link-
ng the Baltic Sea with the Kattegat.

Kjobmannehavn, meaning "merchant's har-
oor", grew into a small town. It spread
westwards over the island of Zealand and
outh on to the small island of Amager. Land
n Amager is still being reclaimed for city use,
nd before long the more distant island of
Saltholm may be used for expansion, if only at
irst for an airport. But till the present century
most of the city was within a small area just
oehind the line of wharves on Zealand. In the
ong harbor there here are large ocean-going
cargo ships alongside the ferry boats to

Helsinki

45

Sweden, Bornholm, Aarhus and other Danish ports. Also by the harbor at the water's edge is the beautiful statue of The Little Mermaid, one of the characters of a Hans Andersen story. Opposite on Amager are the huge ship building yards of Burmeister and Wain.

Most of the people in Copenhagen today live in one of the suburbs to the north or west. They may work in an office, a factory (textile, pottery, beer, etc.) or in a shop. Though the suburbs are served by electric trains, many Copenhageners travel to and fro by bicycle or scooter. Parking them in the city center can cause quite a problem. Midday lunch for the office worker will often be sandwiches – smorrebrod, the well-known Danish open-sandwich on rye bread.

Back at home in the evening the family have their supper together – quite a big meal: fish, meat, eggs and fruit are all popular.

Like many Danes the Copenhageners love the sea: they also love their gardens. So they have no difficulty in finding something to do on the weekend. But no picture of Copenhagen would be complete without a word about Tivoli. This is the large area in the center of the city where many forms of entertainment are found grouped together: a park, boating lake, pantomime, dance hall, orchestral hall, circus, restaurants, etc. No wonder Copenhagen attracts many tourists!

The Danish Parliament and the Royal Palace are also here in the capital city. At one time Copenhagen was the capital of a country which included much more of Scandinavia. The histories of these countries are very complex if only because they are so interwoven. Denmark once extended over Sweden, Norway, Greenland and Iceland; Sweden, once extended over Finland and Norway. Today they are all separate countries except Greenland which since 1953 has been regarded as a part of Denmark.

The Scandinavian countries still have much in common: race, religion, language and way of life vary very little from country to country. One useful ability which many of the Scandinavians also have is that of speaking English. So many of them have to take a part in world trade, and so many of them like to travel, that they are all taught English at school. Apart from those living in the extreme north, the clothes they wear are very similar too – very similar to those worn in Britain or the United States.

To help each other in trade, most Scandinavian countries linked together with Britain and a few other European countries in 1959 to form the *European Free Trade Association* (EFTA). The chief aim of this Association is to reduce the duties on goods which pass between them. This is yet another way in which they are joined together to form the unit which can go by the one name, Scandinavia.

difficult words

Arctic Circle. Latitude 66° 30′ N. At this line on June 21st the sun never sets, and on December 22nd the sun never rises. To the north the number of dark winter days and light summer days increases. These effects are related to the inclination of the earth's axis.

continental shelf. The gently sloping submarine platform bordering a continent. Usual limit taken as 100 fathoms (or 200 meters).

drifting. Fishing with a net which hangs vertically below floats on the sea (typical dimensions: 40 feet depth for 1½ mile length), which thus catches the surface-swimming fish.

echo sounder. An instrument which can be used at sea to detect a shoal of fish. A sound wave is sent down by the instrument and the speed of the returning echo shows on a chart whether the reflection is coming from the sea bed or something (a shoal) nearer the surface.

European Free Trade Area (EFTA). The trading area established in 1959 (Austria, Denmark, Norway, Portugal, Sweden, Switzerland and the United Kingdom) with the aim of lowering trade barriers between the countries concerned.

F.A.O. Food and Agricultural Organization, of the United Nations.

fjord. A valley over-deepened by the action of a glacier. The over-deepening has extended below sea level, and hence, when the ice melts, the sea enters to drown the valley.

glacier. A mass of snow and ice moving down a valley, to give it a broad steep-sided form.

Great Ice Age. The period in geological time when a large portion of the earth was covered by ice (the Pleistocene epoch of the Quaternary period – approximately one million years ago).

grid. Network of lines, e.g. for electricity.

Lapps. The people of northern Scandinavia who for centuries have had the right to move freely over the national frontiers in this area. They probably first came from Siberia via Finland in the 9th Century.

meteorology. The study of the atmosphere in order to forecast the weather.

North Atlantic Drift. The warm ocean current in the North Atlantic, coming from the S.W. as a continuation of the Gulf Stream.

saeter (or seter). A simple upland farm used in the summer months for grazing cattle.

seine. A ring net with lines below which are tightened up to trap in the fish as the net is hauled out of the sea.

territorial waters. The sea areas around a state which are regarded as belonging to the state. The limit decided by different countries varies.

trawling. The type of fishing which uses a bag-shaped net dragged along the sea bed to catch the fish which live low in the water.

Vikings. The people who sailed out from Scandinavia, 8th to 10th Centuries, raiding, exploring, and settling in other areas.